How to be an

Awesome Author!

Written by Sally Odgers
Illustrated by A.C.E. Elisabeth Martin

First Published May 2013

A companion to (Giving Our Kids) A Reason to Write

Isbn 978-1-304-95580-7

How to be an AWESOME AUTHOR

By Sally Odgers

Contents

Introduction

You can write awesome stories. All you need is an idea, some characters, a setting, a plot and—

Whoa there! This is starting to sound like hard work. And you know what? It is hard work, but it can still be fun. In this book you'll find out lots of ways to make those awesome stories even more awesome.

You'll learn about

- Ideas
- Tools
- Beginnings
- Middles
- Ends
- Characters
- Plots and paces
- Settings and periods
- Awesome words
- Not-so-awesome words
- Dialogue
- Editing

And lots and lots more.

So let's get going, shall we?

Why Would You Write a Story?

Writing stories is hard work, so why would you want to write one?

- Maybe you have to write one for school.
- Maybe you have some spare time and you want to have something to show for it.
- Maybe someone gave you an awesome blank book or a notepad or iPad or tablet and you want to use it right now.
- Maybe you have a **grand** idea.
- Maybe something happened to you and you think it would be a good story.
- Maybe something happened and you think it should have happened another way…or happened to someone else… or not at all.
- Maybe you want to be an 

Why not? All authors were kids once. And did you know some people have been authors and kids ***at the same time***?

Some of them have even written BOOKS.

Arthur

If you wrote a book what would you call it? Write down your awesome title before you forget it.

____

Ideas

Ideas are all around you.

Every time you think it would be cool to do something, that's an idea.

Whenever you think, ***What if…?*** that's an idea.

If you think, ***If I had done that,*** or ***if they hadn't done this, then this, that or the other might have happened***—these are ideas.

Ideas often begin with, ***I wish*** or ***If only*** or ***I hope*** or ***I'm scared*** or ***I don't want.***

Of course, ideas don't all have to be about ***I***. They can be about ***you*** or ***him*** or ***her*** or ***they***. They can also be about ***a person*** or ***a dog*** or ***that dragon*** or ***the school*** or ***the old shoe***.

The best ideas are often about unusual things. Look at the list below.

a boy the dog my house a picnic

Dad's car a turkey that dragon

a vase the castle the mouse

the party a carpet the new truck

two birds my holiday *Gran's biscuits (yum)*

All these could be ideas, or subjects for story writing.

The trouble with them is that they are plain and ordinary. If you use plain, ordinary subjects, your stories might be ordinary too. That is sometimes good, but at other times you want a story to be—

Exciting Weird UNUSUAL Different

Scary Sad Surprising Magical

Interesting Funny Silly Creepy

Shiversome... Cacklesome... Adventuriferous!

Hold on – those last three aren't real words, are they? Well, are they? You decide!

(And if they could be words, what would they mean?)

Let's see if we can make some of the ideas in the list more interesting.

A boy in danger A boy with green hair A boy inventor

A boy up a tree A scary boy **An invisible boy**

How's that for a start? You could add lots more.

A boy with a ladder A yelling boy A missing boy

A boy singer A boy on a boat A boy with a clock **A boy in a wig**

A purple boy A boy with six dogs A flying boy **A yob**

Hold on – that last word looks weird. Why? (Hint- try spelling it backwards!)

Often if you use an unexpected word in your idea, the story will be more interesting.

If you think about castles, you probably think of an ***old castle.*** There's nothing wrong with that, but what about ***a gold castle*?** Or ***a wooden castle*?** Or ***a castle in space*** or ***a grass castle?*** A *forgotten castle* is fun and what about *a cackling castle*?

Here are more-

A secret pig A furry fish A plastic rose A house in the sea

The glass cave **The fat tree** A silly elephant Violet jam

A fussy fern A flowery lion A hungry house a sleepy song

Hold on – how can you have a secret pig? Or a hungry house? Why would a boy want a

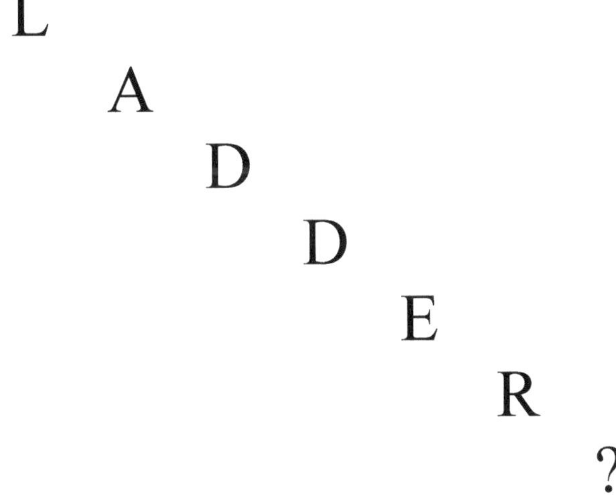

I can think of lots of reasons. Can you? Let's talk about that soon. But for now- let's talk about *writing tools!*

Let's Get Some Writing Tools

What tools do you need to become an

AWESOME AUTHOR?

First you need an awesome imagination. An awesome imagination is an imagination that is awesome. Why is it awesome? Well, it is awesome because it gives you presents ***all the time.***

Great ideas are presents. Really. They come wrapped up in ribbons made of colours and stars and songs and words and memories. But, what do you do with a great idea that just popped into your head?

Matilda

Well, you can just let the idea float about in its own little idea cloud, like a goldfish in a bowl.

It can be your pet idea. You wouldn't believe how many authors have pet ideas. Next time you meet an author, ask him or her this question;

"What's your pet idea, and where do you keep it?"

If you don't want a pet idea, maybe you could tell your grandma, or your best friend, or your teacher about your great idea. Then it becomes a *shared idea.*

Caution! If you *do* tell your grandma or your best friend or your teacher about your great idea, they'll probably nag until you write it into a story. You can't let your fans down.

Maybe you could draw the idea. That's fun. Get out your coloured pencils or your drawing tablet or some paints and make the idea into a picture. You could make it into lots of pictures. Then you could arrange the pictures to make a picture-story.

You could write some words on the pictures and make a comic book, or a graphic novel.

You could write the idea down so it can't float away. Writing an idea down is like putting a sandwich in the refrigerator for later. When you have time, you get it out and eat it… or turn it into a story.

So that's your first story tool.

1. **An awesome imagination.**

What other tools do you need?

A mega memory is useful. Close your eyes right now and –

Oops! If your eyes are closed, you can't read the instructions, can you? Better open them again.

Now you have two choices. Either read the instructions and then carry them out from memory, or get someone to read them aloud to you while your eyes are closed. Maybe the computer can do it. Some computers are pretty smart.

Ready? Now you're either reading ahead or listening to your friend or your sister or your teacher or the computer reading aloud.

Close your eyes right now and think about something that happened this morning. It can be funny, or annoying, or just ordinary, but it has to be something that really happened.

Think about the happening for a few seconds.

Now think about it again, and pay attention to the way things looked, sounded and felt.

Where did it happen?

Was it warm or cold?

If you were inside the house, was there a draft?

Did someone speak?

Did you hear traffic or cows or pigeons or snow or sand falling off a camel's eyelashes?

Of course, if a cross-eyed camel crept in and stole your porridge, (or sliced bananas with strawberry syrup) then you'd know it was *that* breakfast… right?

Hieronymous Beetle
(Cross-eyed and proud of it)

Oops – forget that bit. We're meant to be remembering, not imagining.

Open your eyes and write down everything you remember about the thing that happened this morning.

There's your memory at work. The thing you have just written is called ***a scene.*** It starts at the beginning of the memory and then carries on to the end.

Now, let's try that again. Instead of remembering something that happened this morning, remember something that happened a few days or a few weeks ago.

It will probably have to be something that doesn't happen every day.

If you try to remember breakfast from two Wednesdays ago, how are you going to know if it is *that* breakfast or a different one? I mean, if you eat porridge, or toast, or muesli or muffins or sliced bananas with strawberry syrup every day for breakfast, they sort of blur in to a big super-breakfast, right?

Pick a memory that stands out. It can be-

- arriving at a birthday party
- or the time your friend's kitten scratched you
- or when your neighbour dyed her hair pink.

Hold on – you say your neighbour does that all the time? Okay, what about

- the time her dog got out and she chased it down the footpath in her pyjamas and fluffy bunny slippers?

Think about this memory from a few days or weeks ago until you can picture just how it felt, looked and sounded.

Think about how *you* felt.

Were you nervous? Happy? Looking forward to it?

Did you think it was funny? Did you wish it was your party? Were you cross with the kitten or with your friend? Were you afraid your neighbour might not catch the dog? Did you want to help chase it but your mum said no? Did you laugh until your hat fell off? Now, write down what you remember.

Let's try this for a third time. This time, remember something that happened a long time ago. It might be two years ago or way back when you were a little kid.

It could be so long ago that you think of the *you* it happened to as someone else.

Maybe you were scared of something you like doing now.

Or perhaps you remember eating something you don't like now?

Or eating something you hated but that you've grown to like?

Did you get into trouble for doing something you didn't know was naughty? Or did you try to help someone and make a mistake?

Sometimes you remember doing something that was fun then, but which you know you can't do now.

I expect you're too big to wiggle through the dog door now. You're probably too big to ride on Dad's shoulders. It could be that whatever it was just wouldn't be fun anymore. Little kids like doing some things big kids don't enjoy. Little kids love to bash saucepan lids together. Big kids don't think that's fun. Besides, it makes the screws loose in the lids. The handles fall off and roll about on the floor and even when you screw them back on they keep getting woggly.

Now, write down that memory from when you were a little kid. It might be a bit fuzzy, but try not to make anything up. Try to write down what *did* happen and not what someone told you happened or what you think might have happened.

Good. Now you have written three ***scenes*** from your memory.

Here's something else you can do. Find some other people who were there when one or more of the three memory scenes happened. Without showing them your scenes, ask if they remember what happened. Then ask them to tell you about it or, better still, to write it down.

You can ask ***open-ended*** questions. Here are some examples.

"What do you remember about when we walked into Maddison's party?"

"What did you think about Ms Smith's new car when she first got it?"

"What did we do when we went to Wave Rock when we were little kids?"

"What happened on the day we dog-sat for Cousin Kerry?"

If this doesn't work, you could try asking a closed question first.

"Do you remember when we went to Maddison's party and walked in together?"

"Do you remember when we took the train to Dandenong and I lost something?"

The person you're asking will probably answer either *Yes* or *No.* If it's *Yes,* you can ask another question.

"What do you remember about it?"

"What did I lose?"

When you ask questions like this, you are ***interviewing your witness***. If you interview a lot of people you get lots of different pieces of memory to add to your own.

Some people remember things differently. *You* might remember when your big sister put a dead banana in your lunchbox. *She* might remember putting a nice *ripe* banana in your lunchbox.

You might remember when your little brother got into trouble for feeding his sausage to Aunt Flora's dog at a barbeque. Your brother might remember the dog sneaking up and stealing his sausage. Aunt Flora might remember cleaning up dog-sick on the patio. Mum might remember having to apologise to Aunt Flora afterwards.

If you all write down your memories, and they're different, does that mean someone is telling fibs?

No, it just means they're all remembering the *important* part or *the way it seemed* and that is different for everyone.

What use is a mega memory to an **awesome author**?

Well, the more you remember about real things that happen, the more details you can add to ideas from your awesome imagination. You mix things that really happened (like Aunt Flora cleaning up dog-sick on the patio) with an awesome idea (like having your own pet dragon) and you come up with a funny scene where your character, Princess Maripilla, has to clean up dragon-sick from the marble patio in the *forgotten castle.* And that's **AWESOME!**

So that's your first two story tools.

1. **An awesome imagination**
2. **A mega memory**

What other tools do you need?

The next tool you need is **a logical mind**. What's that? It's a mind that lets you see what would probably happen.

Let's say you know your friend Tyler loves the colour blue. You go to the shop to buy a present for Tyler's birthday. You see two pens with rubber monkeys on the ends. One is blue and the other is pink. Your logical mind tells you which pen to buy for Tyler.

(Hint – it's *not* the pink one…)

Let's say you have a brand new white woollen top. The first time you wear it, your friend Tyler offers you a rainbow ice cream she bought fifteen minutes ago. The bottom of the cone is snapped off and bits of rainbow are drooling out of the end. Your logical mind tells you what is likely to happen if you take that ice cream and try to eat it.

(Hint—it will probably mean your white woollen top will never look quite the same again.)

Let's say Princess Maripilla has a pet dragon with wings and she puts it in a paddock and forgets to feed it. Your logical mind tells you what the dragon is likely to do next… In fact, your logical mind might make all kinds of suggestions! Let's look at some of them below.

up and awayyyyyy…

up

1. The dragon will go up

2. The dragon will sneak into the castle kitchen and eat all the stew…

3. The dragon will fly up to Princess Maripilla's window, zoom in and eat Princess
   Maripilla…
   Or maybe her breakfast

So- there's your logical mind. It's easy to use. Just remember to ask yourself, "What *would* happen?"

This is not the same as asking, "What happens in most stories?"
or "What would I do if I was in Princess Maripilla's position?"

It means, "What *would* happen with *these* characters and *this* situation, in *this* time and place?"

What use is a **logical mind** to an **awesome author**?

Well, using your awesome imagination gives you stories that are exciting and fun to read. Using your logical mind makes your stories *believable* to readers. They'll be waiting to read what happens next and when they have read it they'll think, *well, of course that's what happened! I can totally believe in this awesome story.*

So that's your first three story tools.

1. **An awesome imagination**
2. **A mega memory**
3. **A logical mind**

What other tools do you need?

The next tool you need is **a valiant vocabulary**. What's that? It's a vocabulary that gives you the perfect word for every situation.

What's a vocabulary though? A vocabulary (say it vo-cab-you-larry) is your own private word bank. It's where you store all the awesome words you know or can find out.

Knowing the perfect word for a story or poem is just like having the perfect brick to put in a wall or the perfect shoes for climbing trees.

Sometimes, the perfect word is the first one that jumps out of your mind. More often, you should toss that one away. Just ask Mr Bock. He's the teacher who just wandered into this book.

Well, that's very helpful, Mr Bock. Not.

Awww- cute little puppy…

Is this a good description?
No.
Why not?
Because most pups are little and cute, so this doesn't tell us anything new. "Little" and "cute" are ***weak words.***

Awww- a wriggly velvet puppy

Your valiant vocabulary is an awesome tool. Remember, words don't have to be long and fancy to be valiant. For example, "curt" is a valiant word. So is "berry-red". "Ample" is a valiant word. There are so many valiant vocabulary words it's not possible to fit them all into this book. Maybe it will help if we look at some words that are *not* part of your valiant vocabulary. At least, they shouldn't appear too often.

Nice, silly, pretty, soft, good, bad, little, big, cute, sweet. Why aren't they valiant? Well, they don't tell us anything new or important. Remember the *cute little puppy*? Remember the *wriggly velvet puppy*? Which one gives you a better picture in your mind?

It's not only single words that can be not-so-valiant. There are ready-made phrases that might have been clever the first time someone used them, but are now dull and meaningless.

Think about *white as snow* for example. For one thing, snow is white only when it has just fallen and no one has messed it up or let their dogs wee on it. For another, not many things *are* that white. *White as a sheet* is another example. You sometimes hear or read about someone being *white as a sheet*. How much sense does that make? So, let's take notice of Mr Bock and think about the logic of any description. Does it make sense? Does it tell us something special and new? Is it something other writers haven't used over and over?

You can help your valiant vocabulary along by noting down new words when you find them. Use a dictionary to find out exactly what they mean.

So that's your first four story tools.

1. **An awesome imagination**
2. **A mega memory**
3. **A logical mind**
4. **A valiant vocabulary**

What other tools do you need?

The next tool you need is **a strong finish**. This is really two things. One is the end of your story, which has to be just right. The other is the strength and will to *finish your story properly*. That means writing this story from the beginning to the end, and not rushing off somewhere else in the middle and leaving it unfinished.

OK, maybe Ms Tiggy comes by with her wriggly velvet puppy and you just have to stop and have a cuddle. Then you think up a brand new story idea about the puppy. That's fine, but later, when Ms Tiggy and the puppy have gone home, then you get back to writing your half-done story. When it's properly finished, *then* you can get down to writing *The Tale of the Wriggly Velvet Puppy.*

Ms Tiggy and Jackbeard

So that's your first five story tools.

1. **An awesome imagination**
2. **A mega memory**
3. **A logical mind**
4. **A valiant vocabulary**
5. **A strong finish**

What other tools do you need?

You need **a place to write**.

A place to write might be a table or a desk, or a tablet or laptop. It might be the school library or the garden shed. The perfect place is different for different people.

Some awesome authors write best where there is lots of stuff happening. Others do their best work in a quiet space where no one interrupts. Some authors like to have music playing while they write. Some want it to be really really quiet.

It is easier to write an awesome story if your little sister isn't rubbing mashed banana in your hair.

A place to write includes something to write with. Writing pads are good. So are exercise books. You will also need a ruler and a pencil or a pen. If you use a pencil, make sure you have a pencil sharpener and an eraser too. Computers and tablets are good for writing stories.

So that's your first six story tools.

1. **An awesome imagination**
2. **A mega memory**
3. **A logical mind**
4. **A valiant vocabulary**
5. **A strong finish**
6. **A place to write**

What else do you need?

You need **a place to keep stuff safe**.

Your stories are valuable. They are special, so you want to keep them safe. There are lots of ways to do this. If you write your stories on paper, clip the pages together when you have finished. That way, you won't lose any. Put the pages in a folder, or a document wallet, or a special drawer in a desk.

Sakura

Another way to do it is to write your stories in an exercise book and keep it in the desk or high up on your book shelf so your little brother can't get at it.

If you write your stories on a computer or tablet, make sure you save them properly in the right folder. Don't use a file name like *my story*. That's no help when you're looking for a particular story. Give it a proper title.

If you can't think of one yet you could save it as *Cross eyed Camel* or *Velvet Puppy* or *February 2014.* Save your document before you start to write and make sure you save any changes you want to keep.

So that's your first seven story tools.

1. **An awesome imagination**
2. **A mega memory**
3. **A logical mind**
4. **A valiant vocabulary**
5. **A strong finish**
6. **A place to write**
7. **A place to keep stuff safe**

Check!

Beginnings

Beginnings are important. They are the first step in your story journey. The first thing you need to know about beginnings is that they have to go in the right place.

Yes, of course they go at the start of the story, but where does that story start?

There are three big mistakes you can make with beginnings.

1. The beginning is too early.
2. The beginning is too late.
3. The beginning isn't interesting.

A too-early beginning starts way before anything interesting happens. If your story is about Kayden and the day his adventure started, then don't start the story on the day he first went to school… unless that *is* the day of his adventure. If your story is about how Harrison got lost while holidaying on a tropical island, don't start with Dad saying it would be really good to go on a holiday to a tropical island. Start with the family already there, and then quickly explain how this came about.

Dad said nobody could get lost as long as they could see Captain Cash's Cove. Harrison looked about.

So where was the cove? All he could see was jungly stuff buzzing with insects.

A holiday on a deserted tropical island had seemed such an awesome idea, until now.

A too-late beginning throws the readers right into things so fast they don't have a clue what's going on. Seven names are mentioned and the readers don't know if Pippin is a person, a pixie or a cross-eyed camel. What's more, they never find out.

The beginning of your story should get the readers' attention, so make it sound interesting. Here are ten beginnings of stories. Which ones make you want to read on? Which ones make you want to stop reading?

1.

Jo had a cute little kitten. She liked to play with it. One day she made a ball of wool for the kitten. The kitten liked that.

2.

"I want a pet dinosaur," said Abbie.
"A goldfish would be better," said Tom.
But Abbie wanted a dinosaur.
"We could get you a toy one," suggested Mum.
But Abbie wanted a living dinosaur.

3.

Jasper was climbing the ladder to the loft when his foot slipped.

4.

Pippin had the same name as a hobbit and a kind of apple. No wonder he was amazing.

5.

Kayden first saw the white birds when he went hiking with his brother.
"Look at those birds!" he said.
"What birds?" said Ben, not bothering to look.
That was the trouble with Ben. He never did bother to look.

6.

It was the first day of the holidays. Mara went down to the shop and bought an ice cream. Then she played with her friend Tamika.

7.

"Who wants to come shopping for purple clogs?" asked Mum.

8.

"If 7 X 7 = 49," wrote Ms Jackman on the whiteboard, "what does 7 X 8 =?"

Silence.

"Well, what?" said Ms Jackman, turning to face our class.

Gasps.

"What?" said Ms Jackman again.

Heather put up her hand. "Um- Ms Jackman? Your face is green."

9.

"Slugs for breakfast," said Dad.

"Yay!"

10.

The sun rose over the eastern hills, casting rays over the town. The sky had been grey and now it turned pink and blue. The birds twittered in the trees like sleepy angels. As the sun rose higher in the sky, the trees stood quietly.

Have you made up your mind? Now, take a minute to think about why you feel that way.

Let's look at Beginning 1.

> *Jo had a cute little kitten. She liked to play with it. One day she made a ball of wool for the kitten. The kitten liked that.*

People who like cats and stories without much excitement might want to read on. So might people whose first name is *Jo.* Others – not so much.

Why?

The weak words in this beginning are, *cute, little* and *liked.*

Let's look at Beginning 2.

> *"I want a pet dinosaur," said Abbie.*
> *"A goldfish would be better," said Tom.*
> *But Abbie wanted a dinosaur.*
> *"We could get you a toy one," suggested Mum.*
> *But Abbie wanted a living dinosaur.*

This one is also about a pet, but a pet dinosaur is a lot more unusual than a pet kitten. What readers would find this beginning interesting? Someone interested in dinosaurs might read on.

So would anyone who has ever wanted something and been offered something that wasn't as much fun instead.

Readers know Abbie probably won't get her living dinosaur but there's just a chance she might, so they will probably want to read on and find out how. Even if she doesn't, they'll probably want to know what happens.

How about Beginning 3 then?

Jasper was climbing the ladder to the loft when his foot slipped.

All right! Jasper is climbing a *ladder*. He's going to the *loft*. His foot *slips*. That's three interesting things in a single line. Most people find ladders interesting because they let you reach things that are usually either too high up or too far down. A *loft* is an interesting place because things get stored in there, there's usually a view from the top of the house, and it's a place that doesn't get visited often. A foot slip means a scare at best and a fall at worst.

Let's look at Beginning 4.

Pippin had the same name as a hobbit and a kind of apple. No wonder he was amazing.

Pippin could be a person, or a puppy or a cereal box on legs, but he's *amazing.* Most readers would want to read on to see who and what he is, and just what is amazing about him.

Beginning 5 has a few interesting points to it.

Kayden first saw the white birds when he went hiking with his brother.
"Look at those birds!" he said.
"What birds?" said Ben, not bothering to look.
That was the trouble with Ben. He never did bother to look.

Two brothers are hiking and they clearly don't get on too well. That might make a reader wonder why they have gone out together. But that's not all.

It doesn't just say *Kayden saw white birds*, it says *Kayden **first** saw the white birds*. This makes it sound as if the white birds are important, and Kayden is going to see them again.

Even readers who don't go hiking and are not especially interested in birds might read on to see what will happen.

Here's Beginning 6.

It was the first day of the holidays. Mara went down to the shop and bought an ice cream. Then she played with her friend Tamika.

Most readers have holidays, and most of them like ice cream and spending time with friends. However, most readers would find this beginning dull because it's so ordinary and everyday.

If something interesting is going to happen in this story, it had better happen in the next line or so, or readers will put it aside.

In Beginning 7, shopping is also mentioned.

"Who wants to come shopping for purple clogs?" asked Mum.

Mum is asking a question. She wants to know who wants to go shopping for purple clogs.

The beginning is asking another question. The reader wants to know why Mum thinks ***anyone*** would want to go shopping for purple clogs.

"Who wants to come shopping for purple clogs?" asked Mum.

Beginnings that make readers ask questions work well because if you ask a question, you want the answer.

Here's Beginning 8.

> *"If 7 X 7 = 49," wrote Ms Jackman on the whiteboard, "what does 7 X 8 =?"*
>
> *Silence.*
>
> *"Well, what?" said Ms Jackman, turning to face our class.*
>
> *Gasps.*
>
> *"What?" said Ms Jackman again.*
>
> *Heather put up her hand. "Um- Ms Jackman? Your face is green."*

This is a bit of a tricky one. Some readers would spot the maths problem at the beginning and toss the story aside.

Others would probably stop to ask themselves if they know the answer.

Caspar

Right after the problem is written up, there's a single word sentence. *Silence.* This is a little unusual, so they might read on, especially if they spot the second single-word sentence just underneath. Of course once they know Ms Jackman has a green face the question is in their mind…

Beginning 9 is another one like Beginning 7. It puts the question right away. The second single-word sentence asks another one.

> *"Slugs for breakfast," said Dad.*
> *"Yay!"*

Why would Dad offer someone slugs for breakfast?
Why would anyone think that was a good idea?

How about Beginning 10 then?

The sun rose over the eastern hills, casting rays over the town. The sky had been grey and now it turned pink and blue. The birds twittered in the trees like sleepy angels. As the sun rose higher in the sky, the trees stood quietly.

This is a scene-setting opening and some readers would like it a lot. It is a fairly slow beginning, because instead of questions it throws up word pictures. That asks the reader to stop and imagine each piece of the scene. The sun rises over the hills… but there's a town, so picture that as well. The sky goes from grey to pink and blue. Then add the birds twittering and stop to think about sleepy angels. The sun rises higher and the trees are quiet.

Some readers enjoy word pictures like this one. Others would be annoyed and bored because there's no one in the picture except for the birds. They want action!

So, there are ten beginnings. Maybe you could conduct a poll by reading these out to some of your friends and see who likes which—and why!

Which one would you like to use in a story? Which one would you like to read in a story by someone else? Do you like the same beginning as an **awesome author** as you do as a **ravenous reader**?

Middles

You hope to hook your readers with your beginning by making them think of questions or getting them to see word pictures. How about the middle though?

The middle is the longest part of the story. It's when things happen. Things go wrong, or someone tries to fix something, or goes to do something, or chases a goal. Something always changes in the middle of a story.

An important thing to remember when you write the middle is this.

What promise? That's easy. It's the promise you made in the beginning of the story. Your beginning tells your readers something important about the story. Look at Beginning 5, the one about Kayden, his brother Ben and the white birds.

Kayden first saw the white birds when he went hiking with his brother.

"Look at those birds!" he said.

"What birds?" said Ben, not bothering to look.

That was the trouble with Ben. He never did bother to look.

The promise this beginning makes is that the story is about a boy named Kayden who has a brother called Ben. Kayden sees white birds that *are going to turn out to be important later in the story.*

How do we know that? Because this is *the* ***first time*** *he saw them.* That means he will see them again.

We also know Ben doesn't see the birds and is not interested in them. That suggests Ben has missed out on something important.

How could you break your promise to your readers?

Well, by not delivering the goods. If the story turns out to be about Kayden's and Ben's little sister who has a dolls' tea party while the boys are out hiking, then the promise is broken. If Kayden never sees the white birds again, then the promise is broken. If Ben goes off to visit a mate and plays no further part in the story, then the promise is broken.

Keeping your promise to your readers doesn't mean the story has to go exactly the way they expect. It can have shocks and surprises and twists and turns. It *does* mean things that **seem** important have to **be** important.

The fact that Kayden and Ben have different ways of thinking seems important. The white birds seem important.

Let's look at Beginning 4.

Pippin had the same name as a hobbit and a kind of apple. No wonder he was amazing.

What promises does this one make?

Pippin is amazing. It says so right there in the text. It doesn't say, *Mum thought Pippin was amazing* or *Pippin's little sister thought Pippin was amazing* or even *Pippin believed he was amazing.* No, it says, *No wonder he was amazing.* So, that's the promise in the text. Pippin has got to be amazing.

So, what happens if Pippin is just ordinary in the story? Readers are going to feel cross. It's not that they mind stories about ordinary people, but this time they were promised a story about someone who was *amazing* and that's what they expected to get.

How about Beginning 2? What promises does that one make?

> *"I want a pet dinosaur," said Abbie.*
> *"A goldfish would be better," said Tom.*
> *But Abbie wanted a dinosaur.*
> *"We could get you a toy one," suggested Mum.*
> *But Abbie wanted a living dinosaur.*

It doesn't promise Abbie will get a living dinosaur for a pet. It promises that Abbie will stick to her idea for as long as she can, and that she will do everything she can think of to get hold of that pet dinosaur.

Apart from keeping your promises to your readers, there are other things you can do to make your story-middles awesome. Like the awesome beginnings, these are all about questions. In this case there are four of them.

One is something your readers should be asking.

"What's going to happen next?"

That means they are ***engaged*** and ***interested*** and ***invested*** in the story.

The other three are questions authors should ask themselves.

These three questions give you a perfect balance between a believable story and an exciting story.

Let's look at Beginning 2 again. Abbie wants a pet dinosaur. That's her goal, or problem, in the story. In the beginning two people make suggestions.

1. Tom says she should get a goldfish. This tells us Tom thinks one pet is as good as another, and that Abbie should settle for something easy to get.

2. Mum says she can have a toy dinosaur. This tells us Mum understands it has to be a dinosaur, but since there are no dinosaurs now a toy one is the only option.

Abbie still really wants a living dinosaur.

Let's look at those questions.

Readers: What's going to happen next?

Awesome Author: What *would really* happen?

Awesome Author: What is the most interesting thing that *could* happen?

Awesome Author: What do my readers *want* to happen?

The Readers' question should be answered within the story. The important thing is for the readers to ask it. (Remember, that means they are ***engaged*** and ***interested*** and ***invested*** in the story.)

The first Awesome Author question is the one that ties the story to real life and believability. Let's try to answer it now. What *would* happen to a kid who wanted a pet dinosaur?

In real life, Abbie would not get what she wants. There is no possible way for her to have a living pet dinosaur. She would have to accept that. So, the middle of the story could be about Abbie learning that no matter how much you want something, you can't always have it, and being okay with that.

The second Awesome Author question is the one where imagination steps in. What would be the most interesting thing that could happen?

Well, it would be awesome if Abbie could have her dinosaur pet.

Maybe she could have a robot dinosaur or a lizard that looks like a dinosaur. Maybe she could make a puppet dinosaur.

Maybe she could travel in time, or clone a dinosaur egg, or find one hibernating in a cave, or someone else could travel in time.

Maybe she has a pet dinosaur in a virtual reality game, and loves it so much she wants to stay in the game forever.

Maybe dinosaurs have never really gone extinct. Maybe they're just invisible or really rare?

All these are interesting. The one you pick to use depends on whether you want the story to be a *family realism* story or a *fantasy or science fiction* story.

The third Awesome Author question is about what the readers would like to have happen. This isn't always easy to work out because it depends on the reader! Most readers like things to work out well for the main character in a story. That could either mean Abbie gets what she wants somehow, or else that she doesn't get it but is okay with that.

It's up to you, as an Awesome Author, to keep readers interested in the middle of the story, so don't forget what the story is really about.

It's **not** about dinosaurs. It's **not** about pets. **It's about wanting something that seems impossible.**

Remember, the middle is the BIG part of the story. Don't let it go all saggy and baggy or boring. Don't let an exciting beginning fade into a so-so middle.

Say you start a story with two kids finding a magic door in a forest.

You send them through the magic door. (Maybe that's not what would really happen, but it's the interesting thing and the thing your readers want to have happen.)

Now, the next thing has to be *even better*. Don't have them just wander about or have a picnic and go home again. That's dull. That breaks the promise of the beginning.

Is it ever okay for a story to break the beginning's promise?

Yes, sometimes. It's a way of rescuing a dull beginning. Do you remember Beginning 6?

It was the first day of the holidays. Mara went down to the shop and bought an ice cream. Then she played with her friend Tamika.

This beginning promises a fairly everyday story about an ordinary girl doing ordinary things. Remember, we said that if something interesting is going to happen it had better happen soon? Well, the most interesting thing that can happen to Beginning 6 is for an Awesome Author to break its promise.

It was the first day of the holidays. Mara went down to the shop and bought an ice cream. Then she played with her friend Tamika at the park.

"My fingers are sticking to the slide," said Mara. "The ice cream must have leaked."

Tamika didn't answer.

Mara looked up. "I said—" She didn't finish that sentence. Tamika wasn't there.

Ends

Ends are like beginnings. You have to know where to put them. If you end a story too early, your readers will turn pages because they expect more story. If you end it too late, readers get bored. It's like when you have visitors. You have a lot of fun. You talk and play and draw dragons. Then after a while you've said all there is to say and played all the games and the dragons are starting to look cross and sleepy.

Your visitors keep saying, "It's time I went home…" but somehow they don't go.

You know the feeling. So, don't let your story ending hang around too long or your readers will look as cross and sleepy as the dragons.

Why would an ending go on too long?

Often it's because the author loves hanging out with the characters and doesn't want to leave them.

Often it's because the author doesn't really know *how* to write an ending.

If you love those characters, that's awesome! You can write another story about them next time. You can become a series author!

If you don't really know how to end the story, ask the sorts of questions you asked when you were writing the middle.

What would really happen?

What is the most interesting thing that could happen?

What would the readers want to have happen?

There are some endings that are even worse than too-early or too-late endings. These are endings that don't fit the characters.

Remember Beginning 4? If Jasper was climbing that ladder to the loft because he was looking for the magic flute Great-Great-Grandad Joshua packed away up there in 1919, the ending had better let readers know whether he found it or not. Don't have him just change his mind and never think of it again.

Remember Beginning 6? If Mara's friend disappeared for more than a few minutes don't have Mara just go home.

How about the kids who go through the magic door in the forest? How should that story end?

And don't end an awesome adventure story with Kayden waking up and finding it was all a dream… and then finding a white feather in his hand. Having a character waking up and finding out the story was all a dream is telling your readers the story wasn't important. The only it-was-all-a-dream story endings that work are those where the dream has *changed* the main character in some way.

For example, if Abbie got her pet dinosaur in the story from Beginning 2, then she might find it a big problem to feed, too big to keep in the garden and too dangerous to take to school. If that turned out to be a dream she would have learned that sometimes it isn't good to get what you want and might move on to get a real life pet she could handle.

Characters

The characters are the actors in your story. They're the people or animals the story is about. Characters are fun to create and it's worth doing it properly. One of the main things that makes a story less than awesome is if the characters are dull or impossible to believe in.

You have probably noticed that this book has characters. There are the two teachers, Mr Bock and Ms Tiggy.

Mr Bock **Ms Tiggy**

What do we know about them?

Mr Bock likes it when people think clearly and take notice of what he says. He doesn't like weak words.

Ms Tiggy has a wiggly velvet puppy. She says teachers don't have green faces.

Then there are the writing kids…

Matilda Millagra Derwent

Matilda loves using her imagination and drawing pictures. She thinks about things more often than she says them. She like magic and fantasy.

Arthur Endeavour Andersson

Arthur writes a *lot* of stories. He has bright ideas and he is proud of his work. He takes the time to edit his stories on the computer.

Caspar Bloggingwell Nerd

Caspar always has the answers, and he's not shy about speaking up. He's the kind of pupil Mr Bock likes best.

Sakura Hanako

Sakura is organised and tidy. She's good at explaining *why* things happen.

Hieronymous Beetle

Hieronymous is a cross-eyed camel. He always thinks things are obvious. He likes being a cross-eyed camel and refers to it whenever he can. He's the star of a book Arthur wrote.

Jackbeard is Ms Tiggy's puppy. He is wiggly and velvety. He says he can swim.

The kinds of characters you create depend on the kind of story you're writing. Things to think about:

Age. How old is your character?

Often the exact age doesn't matter, but it's a good idea to decide whether someone is six or nine or fifteen or seventy. People who are six don't talk the same way as people who are sixteen and they usually don't have the same interests.

People who are three might still need a day-time nap sometimes. People who are seven usually don't. People who are ninety often do.

Appearance. What does your character look like?

You don't have to describe every last thing about your character. Remember what Mr Bock said about weak words? Well, one or two or three strong words make a much better picture than a whole page of weak ones. Just describe the things that are important to the story.

If you were describing Sakura, you might say she has black hair held up with chopsticks.

Arthur has bright eyes and sticks his tongue out of the corner of his mouth when he's thinking.

Ms Tiggy has long hair and wears floaty floral dresses.

When describing your characters, think about the way other characters see them. Not all bullies are ugly. Not all clever kids wear glasses. Not all farmers wear overalls. Not all professors have bald heads with a frill of hair around the edges.

Names. What is your character's name?

Names are super-important. If you pick a common name, readers will probably think of people they know who have that name. If you pick an unusual name, people will expect the character to be unusual. If you pick an unusual name that belongs to a famous person, then people will think of that person.

Make sure the name you pick matches the character's age.

Someone called James could be six, sixteen or seventy. Someone called Gladys will probably be at least seventy. Someone called Ava or Ruby will be either a kid or over sixty. Some names like Ava, Ruby and Justus go in and out of fashion. Others, like James, Matthew and Elizabeth and Thomas are always around. Often a name comes into fashion when it's used by a character on television or film.

If you have several characters, make sure their names are not too much alike. If you have a Maria, a Marilyn and a Mimi in the same story readers might get confused.

Personality. What is your character like?

There's no point saying characters are clever or funny or bad-tempered or nervous if they do not behave like that in the story. It's better not to *say* what they're like. Show it instead! Don't say *Helena is very clever.* Show Helena answering a difficult question or inventing a new kind of bicycle.

You can have another character say (or think) what someone is like, though. Remember in Beginning 5 when we met Kayden and his brother?

> *Kayden first saw the white birds when he went hiking with his brother.*
> *"Look at those birds!" he said.*
> *"What birds?" said Ben, not bothering to look.*
> *That was the trouble with Ben. He never did bother to look.*

We're in what's called Kayden's "point of view". That is, we know it's the first time Kayden has seen the birds. We know what Kayden knows. Kayden hears what Ben says, and he thinks *...trouble with Ben. He never did bother to look.*

We are not told "Kayden was the sort of person who noticed things." We *see* him noticing them. We're not told "Kayden was interested in the birds". We *hear* him telling Ben about them even though he knows his brother won't bother to look.

How about Heather in Beginning 8?

"If 7 X 7 = 49," wrote Ms Jackman on the whiteboard, "what does 7 X 8 =?"
Silence.
"Well, what?" said Ms Jackman, turning to face our class.
Gasps.
"What?" said Ms Jackman again.
Heather put up her hand. "Um- Ms Jackman? Your face is green."

We are not told what Heather looks like or how old she is. We're not told, "Heather was the sort of person who said what everyone else was thinking". We *see* her put up her hand and tell Ms Jackman her face is green.

We're not told Ms Jackman is a fairly sharp and impatient teacher either. We *hear* that she is in the three words she says to the class.

"Well, what?"

"Well?"

We don't have any idea what Ms Jackman or Heather or the person telling the story look like either, except that Heather tells us Ms Jackman's face is green.

Who is telling the story? It's not Heather or Ms Jackman. It's someone else in the classroom. How do we know? Because the line doesn't say,

"Well, what?" said Ms Jackman, turning to face ***the*** *class.*

It says,

"Well, what?" said Ms Jackman, turning to face ***our*** *class.*

Is it a boy or a girl? How old? What does she or he look like? What kind of person is this?

The character is probably the same age as Heather, and, because the class is learning times tables, they might be nine or ten years old. This person is observant and notices what people do and say. That's all we know.

Back to Ms Jackman, who is a sharp, impatient kind of teacher. She has a green face. What does this say about her?

It can't always be green, because if it was, the class would be used to it. (They wouldn't gasp when she turns round.) Also, if Ms Jackman's face was always green, Heather wouldn't have mentioned it.

Why would a teacher have a green face?

Maybe she's feeling sea-sick.

Maybe she's really an alien.

Maybe she put a skin-mask on in the shower and forgot to take it off.

Maybe she's playing a joke on the class.

Maybe someone has switched the lighting near the whiteboard so it makes her skin look green.

If one of the first four suggestions is correct, that will say something about Ms Jackman's personality. If someone else switched the lighting, then it won't.

Differences. What are the differences between your characters?

If you have several characters the same age, make sure they don't all sound and act alike. Also, make sure every character has an active part in the story. If there's a character in the story who doesn't do anything, then take him or her out.

Later in this book Ms Tiggy will give you a list of characters you can use in your own stories.

Plots and Paces

Plots are made up of things that happen in a story.

Some of the plot is made up of action.

Action is something that you can see happening. If Jasper climbs the ladder to the loft and slips then falls down, and Grandfather drives him to the hospital, that is action.

If Abbie borrows a time machine from the school laboratory and goes back to dinosaur times to find an egg; that is action.

If Ms Jackman rushes off to the staff bathroom to wash the green stuff off her face, and Heather hides under her desk, that is action.

Action involves someone going somewhere for a particular reason or doing something for a specific result.

Other parts of the plot are made up of character development.

Character development is when a character changes in some way because of things that happen in the story.

If Abbie gets stranded in dinosaur times because the time machine breaks down, then she will realise it was a bad idea to use the time machine. If she accepts this was her own fault and makes an effort to fix it, then her character is developing.

If Abbie finds a dinosaur egg and realises taking it to a different time and place would be unkind, and decides she will give up on her chance to have a pet dinosaur, then that is character development.

When you add action to character development, you get a well-rounded plot.

Pace is the speed at which things happen in the story. Action scenes are usually fast-moving. Character development scenes may be slower. Description and scene-setting, back-story and exposition are slower still.

So – what do those things mean? Don't worry. Mr Bock will explain in the chapter called **Mr Bock's Glossary**.

Pace is important because if a story is too slow, readers get bored. If a story is too fast, readers won't understand what is happening.

Settings and Periods

The setting of a story is the place where things happen. It's the place, or places, the characters live, or where they go. Settings are important to most stories. In fact, some stories can happen *only* in some settings.

The more important the setting is to a story, the more it has to be described.

In the ten beginnings, only one of them (Beginning 10) had a description of the setting, and that beginning was *all* setting.

What can we tell about where the other beginnings were set? Let's look at them one by one.

1.

Jo had a cute little kitten. She liked to play with it. One day she made a ball of wool for the kitten. The kitten liked that.

This one is probably set in the house or flat (and maybe the garden) where Jo lives. Apart from that it could be anywhere; we have no idea if it's in the country, the city or a small town. We don't know what country it is, or whether it is summer or winter.

2.

"I want a pet dinosaur," said Abbie.
"A goldfish would be better," said Tom.
But Abbie wanted a dinosaur.
"We could get you a toy one," suggested Mum.
But Abbie wanted a living dinosaur.

This one might be at the place where Abbie lives, or maybe Mum, Tom and Abbie are at the pet shop or in the car. If the story went on for a few more lines the setting might be mentioned. Is the setting important? It could be, if Abbie needs to go to specific places to try and get a dinosaur.

3.

Jasper was climbing the ladder to the loft when his foot slipped.

All we know about this setting is that Jasper is in a building that has a loft and a ladder. It might be his house, or a relative's place. It could be a friend's house or maybe it belongs to a stranger and Jasper shouldn't be there.

4.

Pippin had the same name as a hobbit and a kind of apple. No wonder he was amazing.

This one gives no clue at all.

5.

Kayden first saw the white birds when he went hiking with his brother.

"Look at those birds!" he said.

"What birds?" said Ben, not bothering to look.

That was the trouble with Ben. He never did bother to look.

Since Kayden and Ben are out hiking, they are probably in the country but that's all we know.

6.

It was the first day of the holidays. Mara went down to the shop and bought an ice cream. Then she played with her friend Tamika.

Mara goes to the shop, so she's probably in a town.

7.

"Who wants to come shopping for purple clogs?" asked Mum.

This is probably in a town or a city, since Mum mentions shopping.

8.

"If 7 X 7 = 49," wrote Ms Jackman on the whiteboard, "what does 7 X 8 =?"

Silence.

"Well, what?" said Ms Jackman, turning to face our class.
Gasps.
"What?" said Ms Jackman again.
Heather put up her hand. "Um- Ms Jackman? Your face is green."

This takes place in a classroom with a whiteboard.

9.

"Slugs for breakfast," said Dad.
"Yay!"

This is most likely in a kitchen, but it could possibly be a motel or restaurant and Dad is being funny.

10.

The sun rose over the eastern hills, casting rays over the town. The sky had been grey and now it turned pink and blue. The birds twittered in the trees like sleepy angels. As the sun rose higher in the sky, the trees stood quietly.

This one, as mentioned before, is *all* setting.

The fact that setting is hardly mentioned in nine of these beginnings doesn't mean setting won't play a strong part in the stories. It just means it hasn't been mentioned *yet.*

Let's look at two of the beginnings and put in some clues about setting.

"Who wants to come shopping for purple clogs?" asked Mum.

Amy and I wrinkled up our noses. We expected to spend our island holiday swimming and beachcombing, not shopping.

"We could go to the village market," said Mum. "We could buy some coconuts and mangos."

The sea swished on the sand as we thought about that. Coconuts and mangos sounded good.

Pippin had the same name as a hobbit and a kind of apple. No wonder he was amazing.

'Pippin is amazing!' That's what everyone said. Of course, since he lived in a tiny town tucked in among the Dandenong Ranges, "everybody" didn't add up to many people.

After today, things would be different.

"You're lucky," said his friend Grant. "You get to fly to Sydney and sing in the Opera House."

Pippin nodded. His mouth went dry. He could be amazing in his tiny town, but being amazing in the Sydney Opera House might not be so easy.

These settings make quite a difference to the story beginnings. Now we see Mum wants to buy purple clogs because she's on holiday. Maybe she forgot to bring some cool shoes. Or maybe she saw the purple clogs at the market the day before and has decided to go back and buy them.

Because of the setting, we know how Pippin is amazing (he's an awesome singer) and we also see how coming from a small town might make it difficult to go on feeling amazing when he goes to a busy city. Singing in front of friends and relatives would be different from singing in front of a crowd of strangers at the Sydney Opera House.

On the next page, Ms Tiggy has a list of settings you might use in stories. See if any of them give you awesome ideas.

Ms Tiggy's List of Splendid Settings

the beach	a cove	a factory
on a ship	a sunken city	Ireland
on an island	a village	a magic island
under the sea	a mountain	a lake
a pyramid	a valley	a tree house
a big city	boarding school	a stable
a spaceship	an old mansion	a snowstorm
a farm	a ghost town	a haunted house
a castle	a mine	a secret garden
a desert	a bus	a secret town
a cabin	shopping centre	a locked room
a jungle	a cruise ship	inside a clock
the bush	a dog show	a marsh
a forest	swim carnival	a maze
a palace	a pony trek	a coral reef
a library	an empty school	inside a painting
a small kingdom	a strange planet	a stable
a school	a submarine	a graveyard
a park	a carnival	an attic
a riverbank	a museum	a snowstorm
a cave	an old orphanage	jungle

The period of a story is the year it is set.

The ten beginnings don't give many clues to the time. Beginning 8 mentions a whiteboard and names the teacher *Ms Jackman* so it can't be set before the 1960s. Whiteboards weren't invented until then and before the 1960s Ms Jackman would have been called Miss Jackman or Mrs Jackman.

Pippin has the same name as a hobbit, so the story can't be set before the 1950s when the first story about hobbits was written.

If you plan to set a story in any year but the current one, you will need to do some research.

You can set a story in just about any time as long as you know a bit about it. If you don't know if something was around in 1678 or 2005 or 17BCE, then you can do some research to find out. Of course, if you set your story in the future you can have a lot of fun guessing!

You don't have to say what year you are using, but if it's not now you can put some clues in the story. Let's look at two of the beginnings and add some clues about period.

> *"Who wants to come shopping for purple clogs?" asked Mum.*
> *Amy and I stared at her.*
> *"What are clogs?" asked Amy.*
> *"They were wooden shoes people used to wear on Earth," said Mum.*
> *"Shoes aren't made of wood," I said.*
> *"They used to be, once upon a time," said Mum.*
> *What's wood?" asked Amy.*
> *"Don't you know anything?" I said. "Wood is what trees are made of."*
> *"What's trees?"*
> *Mum sighed. "Maybe you need a history lesson."*

This tells us the story is set a long way in the future, because Mum, Amy and the girl telling the story are not on Earth and it's been so long since they, or their family, left that Amy doesn't know what trees are.

Jasper was climbing the ladder to the loft when his foot slipped.

"Take care, boy!" snapped the butler. "If you do not fetch the candles quickly there will be no light for Mistress Price's supper party."

Jasper caught his breath and went on climbing, taking more care as he placed his stiff leather boots on the rungs. Until he came to be a scullery boy at Hillside Manor, he had never worn shoes in all his nine years of life.

Jasper is nine years old, and is working as a scullery boy. He has never worn shoes and now he has to wear stiff leather boots. Candles are the only way of lighting in a rich house. This can't be nowadays.

Awesome Words and Not So Awesome Words

We talked about words a bit in the Tools chapter when we looked at our Valiant Vocabulary and when Mr Bock talked about weak words.

Weak words are the ones that have been used so much they've lost their impact.

Sweet, little, fluffy, cute, big, nice, quite, good, bad and old are all weak words. They get even weaker when authors use them in phrases without even thinking.

A little old man, a cute little puppy, a big smile, a nice day, a hot dinner, a cosy cottage, a fluffy kitten and an old lady are weak descriptions. Instead of using these descriptions that have been used thousands of times before, think about the thing or person you are describing.

If you come up with a more awesome word or description use that. If you decide you really *do* mean the cottage was cosy and was no particular colour or size or material, then go ahead and use *cosy cottage*. If you decide it is made of stone and the roof is a bit crooked, then put *stone cottage with a crooked roof.* That gives you a more interesting picture.

The tricky thing about using awesome words is that sometimes writers use them in the wrong place. The word *retrieved* is an awesome word. It means *brought back.*

You can say *Ms Tiggy threw the ball and Jackbeard retrieved it.*

Or you could say, *Tom went to his suitcase and retrieved his blue socks.*

However, it you say, *Mr Bock retrieved a present from Ms Tiggy,* it sounds odd. It would be better to say, *Mr Bock* ***received*** *a present from Ms Tiggy.*

The problem with some awesome words like *retrieved* is they mean something exact. If authors use them for any other meaning they sound wrong. The word *scaled* means *climbed something steep.* You can say, *James scaled the cliff* or *Jasper scaled the ladder* but if you say *Gina scaled the road* it sounds odd.

One place a lot of writers misuse words is when they write dialogue. We'll look at this problem in the chapter about dialogue.

Dialogue

Dialogue is the name we give to things characters say in stories.

Dialogue is useful for giving us information about the characters, and for breaking up long stretches of narrative. Here are some things to remember.

Make your characters sound right for their age, period and setting.

Make sure what they say is important to the story. Don't have them chat away about things that don't matter.

Learn how to set dialogue out properly on the page.

Learn the difference between *speech tags* and *action tags* and why ***"said" is king***!

Each new piece of dialogue from a new speaker begins a new paragraph.

Business belongs on the same line as that speaker's dialogue.

This might sound difficult but it's quite easy if you take it step by step.

If you look at a chapter book or a novel, you'll see some lines begin a little way further in from the left-hand margin. Every time that happens, you have a new paragraph beginning.

We've already seen some paragraphs when we expanded some of those beginnings to show period or setting. Here's one now.

Jasper was climbing the ladder to the loft when his foot slipped.

"Take care, boy!" snapped the butler. "If you do not fetch the candles quickly there will be no light for Mistress Price's supper party."

Jasper caught his breath and went on climbing, taking more care as he placed his stiff leather boots on the rungs. Until he came to be a scullery boy at Hillside Manor, he had never worn shoes in all his nine years of life.

This piece of text has three paragraphs in it.

The first one and the third one are *narrative paragraphs.* That is, they give action and exposition. *Action* is someone doing something active and *exposition* is the story explaining how something came to be.

The second paragraph is a dialogue paragraph. It has two bits of dialogue and a speech tag. Both bits are spoken by the butler. No one else says anything in between, so they both belong in the same paragraph.

Let's look at that again. The bits of this text will be shown so you can identify them at a glance.

Action

Dialogue

Exposition

DIALOGUE TAG

Jasper was climbing the ladder to the loft when his foot slipped.

"Take care, boy!" SNAPPED THE BUTLER. **"If you do not fetch the candles quickly there will be no light for Mistress Price's supper party."**

Jasper caught his breath and went on climbing, taking more care as he placed his stiff leather boots on the rungs. Until he came to be a scullery boy at Hillside Manor, he had never worn shoes in all his nine years of life.

If Jasper or the butler said something after the last line, then that would go in another paragraph.

Jasper was climbing the ladder to the loft when his foot slipped.

"Take care, boy!" snapped the butler. "If you do not fetch the candles quickly there will be no light for Mistress Price's supper party."

Jasper caught his breath and went on climbing, taking more care as he placed his stiff leather boots on the rungs. Until he came to be a scullery boy at Hillside Manor, he had never worn shoes in all his nine years of life.

"Hurry!" said the butler.

"I am hurrying, sir," said Jasper. He put his foot on another rung.

So, that is the way to set out dialogue. Look carefully at the lines of dialogue and their tags to see how the punctuation works.

"Take care, boy!" snapped the butler. "If you do not fetch the candles quickly there will be no light for Mistress Price's supper party."

"Hurry!" said the butler.

"I am hurrying, sir," said Jasper.

The dialogue tags (*snapped the butler, said the butler,* and *said Jasper*) are part of the dialogue sentence they attach to. That's why *said* and *snapped* don't have capital S at the beginning and why *sir* has a comma after it instead of a full stop.

If *said Jasper* and *snapped the butler* are both ***speech tags***, what's an ***action tag***?

An action tag is something you use instead of a speech tag. It doesn't have the word *said*, or *asked* or *muttered* or any of those other "said" words in it. Instead, it has some action. That is, the person who was speaking *does* something.

We'll look at that scene again. This time, the speech tags will be replaced by action tags.

Jasper was climbing the ladder to the loft when his foot slipped.

"Take care, boy!" The butler sounded angry. "If you do not fetch the candles quickly there will be no light for Mistress Price's supper party."

Jasper caught his breath and went on climbing, taking more care as he placed his stiff leather boots on the rungs. Until he came to be a scullery boy at Hillside Manor, he had never worn shoes in all his nine years of life.

"Hurry!" The butler tapped his black-shod toe.

"I am hurrying, sir." Jasper put his foot on another rung.

It is easy to tell who is speaking. The difference between speech tags and action tags isn't *only* that one uses a "said word" and the other uses action. Remember how we said speech tags are part of the dialogue sentence, so don't start with a capital letter? Well, action tags are *not* part of the dialogue sentence, and so they *do* start with a capital letter. In fact, an action tag is a whole sentence on its own.

"I am hurrying, sir." Jasper put his foot on another rung. RIGHT
"I am hurrying, sir," Jasper put his foot on another rung. WRONG
"I am hurrying, sir," said Jasper. RIGHT
"I am hurrying, sir." Said Jasper. WRONG

Why *said* is King of the Speech Tags.
Well, why *is* "said" king?

That's the point. It doesn't have much impact because not much impact is needed. The thing about *said* is that it is clear and plain. Listen to people talking. Most of them *say* things or *ask* things. There are lots and lots and lots of other "said words" but how often do you hear them in normal conversation? Here are just a few…

Asked. This is *only* for questions and you hear it quite a lot in real life and in books.
"What's the capital of Australia?" asked Tom.

Answered. This is just for answering questions.
"The capital of Australia is Canberra," answered Mum.

Explained. This is for telling someone some information.
"We can't go until Grandpa is ready," explained Mum.

Yelled. A yell is loud. There are only two reasons to yell dialogue. One is to force someone to hear because you are angry or frightened.
"Stop! There's a car coming!" yelled Tom, grabbing his little sister by the arm.
The other is when speaking to someone a long distance away.
"Dad! Dinner's ready!" yelled Polly across the paddocks.

Shouted, Screamed, Shrieked. The same as yelled.

Cried. This doesn't mean the sobbing, tear-dripping kind of crying. It's an old-fashioned word for a loud excited tone of voice.
"Oh, I'm so glad to see you!" cried Jessie.

Muttered. This is a very quiet way of saying something. It's usually used when you don't want someone else in the room to hear.
"I'm so tired of this," muttered Jake as Mr Bock went on and on about weak words.

Murmured. The same as muttered.

Mumbled. This is similar to muttered and murmured but it usually means not speaking clearly.
"Stop mumbling," said Mum when Josh answered her with his mouth full.

Exclaimed. This is saying something because you are very surprised or making a strong point.
"So that's where it is!" exclaimed Mum when her knitting turned up in the dog's bed.

"I knew it!" exclaimed Jenna.

Grumbled. This means complaining about something.
"It's hardly stopped raining for three days," grumbled Mia.

Complained, Griped, Moaned, Groaned. The same as grumbled.

Whispered. This is the very quietest way of saying something. The only sound is a kind of breathy noise. If you whisper, only someone *very* close to you can hear.
"I'll just creep out so I don't wake the dog," whispered Evie.

Interrupted. This means dialogue cutting across what someone else is saying.
"I just think it would be—" began Jane.
"Not that again!" interrupted Shelley.

Snapped, snarled, growled, grumped, twittered, squawked, squealed, hissed, roared, whined, barked, bleated, sniped, whinged, erupted, grizzled, yelped…

These are all "said words" that don't really mean what they say. To snap means to say something sharply. To snarl or growl is to say something in a cross tone. Grumping is like grumbling, twittering means to talk in a high anxious way…and so on. Most of these words really belong to animals, but you can use them now and then in dialogue. Again, they are very specific.

Here are some more specific "said" words.
Panted, puffed, sobbed, sighed, gasped
These are just about possible.
"I thought I'd never get here," panted Richard.

Here are some unusual words. They are awesome, but you have to know exactly what they mean and how to spell them and you can't use them very often.

Expostulated, conceded, intimated, harangued, interpolated, responded, asserted.

Now we come to some "said words" that aren't just specific or unusual but *wrong.*
Smiled, laughed, grinned, gritted
You *can't* smile, laugh, grin or grit words, so your characters shouldn't either.

Even a cross-eyed camel can see that.

Voices and Tenses

There are lots of different meanings for the word *voice*, but the one we're talking about in this chapter is to do with the person telling the story.

You might say the person telling the story is the author, but the author mostly uses someone else's point of view to present the story. Remember on Page 51 when we talked about the Beginning 5 being told from Kayden's point of view?

The main points of view in story writing are these:

First Person

Second Person

Third Person Limited

Third Person

Omniscient

First Person point of view means one person is telling the story.

Beginning 8 is a First Person beginning. Remember, the person telling the story said *our class*, not *her class* or *their class* or *the class.*

If someone is telling the story as if it happened to him or her, then that is First Person narrative.

Second Person point of view is rare. This is when the person telling the story is addressing the main character as "you".

Third Person Limited is when the author tells us what the main character sees and thinks and feels, but only what the other characters do and say.

Third Person can also be used to tell stories from several points of view. We spend one scene with the first character and the next scene with a different one.

Omniscient point of view is when all the different points of view are in the story without having to wait for the next scene. The author also tells readers things the characters don't know.

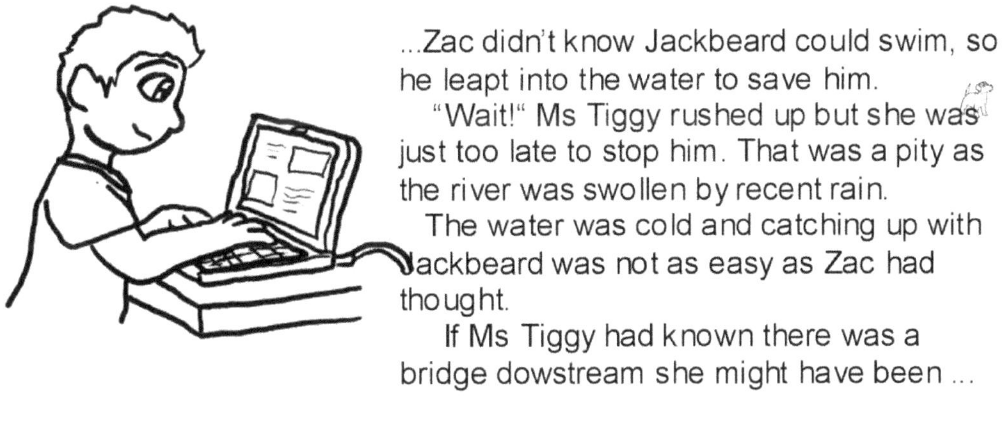

...Zac didn't know Jackbeard could swim, so he leapt into the water to save him.

"Wait!" Ms Tiggy rushed up but she was just too late to stop him. That was a pity as the river was swollen by recent rain.

The water was cold and catching up with Jackbeard was not as easy as Zac had thought.

If Ms Tiggy had known there was a bridge dowstream she might have been ...

Tense is *when* a story is happening.

This doesn't mean what year it is happening, but whether it is happening *now* or has *just* happened or happened a long time ago or will happen in the future.

These are called:

Present tense

Immediate Past tense

Past tense

Future tense

In **Present tense**, the story is happening as it is being told.

Here is a scene written in present tense. You'll be reading it twice over. The first time it is written in First Person, and the second time, in Third Person Limited.

Beginning 8 in First Person, Present tense.

"If 7 X 7 = 49," writes Ms Jackman on the whiteboard, "what does 7 X 8 =?"

Silence.

"Well, what?" says Ms Jackman, turning to face our class.

Gasps.

"What?" says Ms Jackman again.

Heather puts up her hand. "Um- Ms Jackman? Your face is green."

I hold my breath. Heather is right, of course, but what will Ms Jackman do now?

Beginning 8 in Third Person Limited, Immediate Past tense.

"If 7 X 7 = 49," wrote Ms Jackman on the whiteboard, "what does 7 X 8 =?"

Silence.

"Well, what?" said Ms Jackman, turning to face the class.

Gasps.

"What?" said Ms Jackman again.

Heather put up her hand. "Um- Ms Jackman? Your face is green."

Justin held his breath. Heather was right, of course, but what would Ms Jackman do now?

The other kind of Past tense, which is not "immediate", tells about things that happened a while ago and which have now finished happening.

Future tense is as rare as Second Person point of view. Let's look at that passage using both those rare forms.

"If 7 X 7 = 49," Ms Jackman will write on the whiteboard, "what does 7 X 8 =?"

There will be silence.

"Well, what?" Ms Jackman will turn to face your class.

Gasps.

"What?" Ms Jackman will say again.

Heather will put up her hand. "Um- Ms Jackman? Your face is green."

You will hold your breath. Heather will be right, of course, but what will Ms Jackman do next?

Using Second Person is difficult and some readers don't like it.

Using Future tense is difficult and some readers don't like it.

Using Present tense can be difficult… and some readers don't like it.

The easiest and most popular ways to tell a story are probably First Person and Third Person limited, both in immediate Past tense.

Punctuation works as signposts in your story. Here are some common (and not so common) punctuation marks. If you learn to use these well, readers will find your awesome stories much easier to read.

A full stop is also sometimes called a **period.** . That's the dot at the end of a sentence. It shows readers that the sentence is finished.

An ellipsis is three dots close together … It's used to show dialogue or thoughts that trail off without being finished.

"I was thinking…" said Jane.

An **em-dash** is a line. – It is used to show dialogue or thoughts that are suddenly interrupted.

"I was thinking—" Jane broke off when the doorbell rang.

A **comma ,** tells readers to pause a tiny bit after reading the word before it. Two of them are used to divide off part of a sentence if the parts outside the commas will still make sense.

The birds twittered, the breeze blew, and the water rippled.

A **semicolon ;** can be used to join up two short sentences instead of using a conjunction.

We drove down a rough road; it looked as if no one had been here for months.

If you used a comma + conjunction instead, this sentence would look like this.

We drove down a rough road, which looked as if no one had been here for months.

A **colon :** divides off a list from the beginning of a sentence.

We had lots of fruit: pears, peaches, apples, bananas and plums.

A **question mark ?** shows that someone is asking a question.

What is his name?

An **exclamation mark !** shows that someone is exclaiming.

“I knew it!” said Jenna.

An **interrobang ?!** is used only occasionally. It is a cross between an exclamation mark and a question mark.

“She said *what*?!” cried Flora.

Parentheses ( ) divide off a piece of a sentence that is an aside.

We were going to our aunt’s place (well, it was our uncle’s place too) for the summer holidays.

Quote marks come in two sorts; double “ ” and single ‘ ’ . These are used to show dialogue or someone quoting something someone else said.

“I’m going to the skate bowl,” said Flora. “I’m an awesome skater.”

“Careful,” said Angus. “You know what they say; ‘Pride goes before a fall’.”

Sometimes these are used the other way round, like this:

‘I’m going to the skate bowl,’ said Flora. ‘I’m an awesome skater.’

‘Careful,’ said Angus. ‘You know what they say; “Pride goes before a fall”.’

Apostrophes ' have two uses. One is to show some letters are missing from a contraction. (A contraction is a word made up out of two others.)

Here are three contractions. Underneath are the words without the missing letters.

He can't go. We wouldn't let him. It's dangerous.

He cannot go. We would not let him. It is dangerous.

He can~~no~~t go. We would n~~o~~t let him. It ~~i~~s dangerous.

The other use for an apostrophe is to show that someone or something owns something. If there is one owner, then the apostrophe goes *before* the s. If there is more than one owner, then it goes *after* the s.

That's the dog's bowl.

Those are the dogs' bowls.

Annie's hair was curly.

The two girls' hair was curly.

Sometimes you get something called a *collective noun.* That's a thing made up of other things. A team, a crew and a family are all collective nouns. Collective nouns act like single owners.

The crew's ship was in port.

These are the only reasons to use apostrophes. If there are no letters missing and if something doesn't belong to someone, then never use an apostrophe.

More Awesome Words

Here are some more awesome words.

Verbs are action words. They are all about doing.

Strong verbs have more impact than weak ones. A strong verb can usually replace two or three words in a sentence.

Walked is an ordinary verb. Authors often jazz it up by adding an **adverb**, which is a word that describes a verb.

Walked slowly. *Walked* is the verb. *Slowly* is the adverb. It tells us how the character walked.

There is nothing wrong with *walked slowly.* It puts a picture in your head of someone walking at a slow speed.

But, there are stronger verbs that *mean* "walked slowly". Let's look at some of these.

If we make a sentence with *walked slowly* we might get this:

Andrew walked slowly down the road.

Now look at the same sentence with the verb and the adverb replaced by a strong verb.

Andrew strolled down the road.

Andrew rambled down the road.

Andrew wandered down the road.

Andrew dawdled down the road.

Andrew ambled down the road.

Andrew sauntered down the road.

If Andrew was going faster, we could say;

Andrew walked quickly down the road.

We could also change the verb + adverb combination with another stronger verb.

Andrew marched down the road.

Andrew strode down the road.

That sentence rhymes, which might not be what we want, so we can either change “road” to “track”, “path”, “carriage-way”, “highway” or “street”, or change “strode” to “hurried”.

Andrew hurried down the road.

Andrew strode down the track.

Before we leave Andrew and the road, let’s look at some other strong verbs he might use instead of walking quickly, slowly, smartly, nervously, awkwardly and so on.

Ambled, Bustled, Careened, Crept, Danced, Edged, Galloped, Hustled, Idled, Limped, Marched, Meandered, Pottered, Rushed, Sauntered, Scooted, Scuttled, Scurried, Skipped, Slouched, Sneaked, Staggered, Tottered, Trotted.

All of these ways of moving mean something a little different, so spend some time to think of exactly which one you want to use.

There are even more ways Andrew could go down the road!

If it's been raining, he could *squelch* or *splash* down the road. If he's tired or very old, he could *shuffle* down the road. If he's athletic, he might *cartwheel* down the road.

Because strong verbs have strong meanings, don't use "crept quietly", or "rushed quickly", because crept *means* "moved quietly" and rushed *means* "moved quickly".

Because strong verbs have so much impact, don't make every verb in your story a strong one. That would be like adding mustard, jalapeno, chilli, honey, pepper and curry to your sandwich.

Nouns are naming words.

Tables, flowers, dogs, cars, jigsaw puzzles and freckles are all *concrete* nouns. They're called *concrete* nouns not because they're made of cement, but because they are solid. You can see and touch them.

Fear, dreams, thoughts, anger, joy, life, song and sound are all *abstract* nouns. They are not solid and we can't see or touch them.

When using nouns, you often have a choice between ordinary words and specific words.

Bird, vehicle, building, dog, tree, clothes and flower are ordinary words.

Sparrow, duck, lark, pigeon, ute, truck, motorbike, canoe, bulldog, terrier, spaniel, oak, wattle, pine, ash, jeans, coat, tee-shirt, rose, pansy, violet, daisy and orchid are all specific words.

Usually, the more specific words you use, the better picture readers will get when they read your story.

Words that describe nouns are called adjectives.

Adjectives include yellow, gritty, tiny, warm, big, soft, hairy, scary, squelchy, dry, ragged, new and purple.

Adjectives help make specific nouns even more specific!

Let's look at some paragraphs and how they change when we use specific, weak and ordinary words.

"Maripilla, clean up after your pet," said a woman.
Maripilla went to clean up.
"That was naughty," she said to her pet.
The pet took no notice.

"Maripilla, clean up after your dragon," said Doris.
Maripilla ambled away to clean up the marble patio.
"That was naughty," she scolded Gemfire.
The golden dragon ignored her.

"Maripilla, clean up after your messy dragon," shrieked Doris, the plump cook angrily.

Maripilla ambled slowly away to clean up the polished white marble patio.

"That was awfully naughty," she scolded Gemfire crossly.

The golden dragon with the shiny scales took no notice and ignored her.

That version is much too overdone.

"Maripilla, clean up after your dragon," said the cook.

"All right, Doris," said Maripilla. She hitched up her skirts and scurried away to the marble patio where her pet was supposed to be resting.

"That was naughty," she scolded Gemfire as she bundled charred bedding into a pile.

The golden dragon huffed a smoke ring and ignored her.

Here's the last version again with the strong verbs **bolded.**

Maripilla, clean up after your dragon," said the cook.

"All right, Doris," said Maripilla. She **hitched** up her skirts and **scurried** away to the marble patio where her pet was supposed to be resting.

"That was naughty," she **scolded** Gemfire as she **bundled** charred bedding into a pile.

The golden dragon **huffed** a smoke ring and **ignored** her.

Here are the strong adjectives bolded.

Maripilla, clean up after your dragon," said the cook.

"All right, Doris," said Maripilla. She hitched up her skirts and scurried away to the **marble** patio where her pet was supposed to be resting.

"That was naughty," she scolded Gemfire as she bundled **charred** bedding into a pile.

The **golden** dragon huffed a smoke ring and ignored her.

…and here are specific words.

Maripilla, clean up after your **dragon**," said the **cook**.

"All right, Doris," said Maripilla. She hitched up her **skirts** and scurried away to the marble **patio** where her pet was supposed to be resting.

"That was naughty," she scolded Gemfire as she bundled charred **bedding** into a pile.

The golden dragon huffed a smoke ring and ignored her.

That's a long way from the version with the ordinary and weak words, don't you think?

"Maripilla, clean up after your pet," said a woman.

Maripilla went to clean up.

"That was naughty," she said to her pet.

The pet took no notice.

Editing

Editing is something we do to make awesome stories even better.

We already did some editing in the More Awesome Words chapter. Changing weak words into specific words and putting in and taking out adverbs and adjectives is editing.

Editing can be about fixing mistakes in the plot. Sometimes characters change as you write, so by the end of the story you realise your main character wouldn't really have acted the way you had planned out.

Editing is also about fixing mistakes in sentences. Sometimes it means changing words. Sometimes it means cutting some out or adding more. It's all about making stories clear and easy to read *and* about giving readers those awesome word pictures.

Editing is about fixing little mistakes called inconsistencies, too. These happen when you mention in the first page that Emily has short hair and three pages on she suddenly has long hair. Or that Jack is two years older than Jasper on Page 1 but later on Jack is 11 and Jasper is 10.

We're going to take a piece of writing and then edit it so you can see just how this process works. This is based on the story beginning we saw back on Page 26.

The first thing to do is to read through this piece. See where you think it could be edited to make it better.

"Mr Pilgrim will take up to the island on Friday and pick us up a weak later," dad said. "Well have a whole seven days to explore all the bay's."

"Sounds excelent!"Harrison spoke.

Harrison thought he and Dad would explore toogether. Only on the second day dad decides to go fishing. "You can explore," he tells Harrison.

"I might get lost." Said Harrison.

"You can't get lost while you can see Captain Cash's Cove", Dad told.

Harrison wondered around the island. He got hungry.

"I'll go back to dad," he thought. "I just have to find Captain Cod's Cove."

Harrison looked up at the sun. He knew how to find east. Was the cove east or west?

He tried to remember if Mr Pickering, who bought them to the island, had said anything about that.

"OK, I'll climb up a tree and see if I," he yelled.

He climbs the tree and saw the camp.

"That was an adventure, dad, he complained when he got back.

Did you find some places to edit? (Hint- there are more than *20* mistakes!)

Read through the piece again (you can photocopy or print it out) and then do some editing with a pencil. Then read on and we'll look at the piece sentence by sentence the way an editor would.

All right! Here is the first sentence.

"Mr Pilgrim will take ***up*** *to the island on Friday and pick us up a* ***weak*** *later,"* ***dad*** *said.*

The fifth word is wrong. It should be *us*, not *up*.
The sixteenth word is wrong. It should be *week*, not *weak*.
The eighteenth word is wrong. That should be *Dad,* not *dad.*
Did you get all those?
By the way, *up, weak* and *dad* are all real words, but they're not the proper ones to use in this sentence.

*"**Well** have a whole seven days to explore all the **bay's.**"*

The first word is wrong. It should be *We'll*, not *Well.*
The last word is wrong. It should be *bays*, not *bay's.*
Did you get those?
By the way, *Well* and *bay's* are real words, but they're not the proper ones to use in this sentence. Here's a sentence that uses them properly.
"Well," said Dad, "this bay's sand is the whitest I've ever seen."

*"Sounds **excelent!"Harrison** **spoke**.*

The second word is wrong. It should be *excellent,* not *excelent.*
There is no word spelled *excelent.*
The last word is wrong. Of course *spoke* is a word, but it can't be used here. The word should be *said* or *exclaimed.*
There should be a space between the second quote mark and the name, *Harrison.*

*Harrison thought he and Dad would explore **toogether**.*

The last word is wrong. There's no such word as *toogether.* It should be *together.*

***Only** on the second day **dad decides** to go fishing.*
This sentence is clumsy. It really should be attached to the one before it using a conjunction, *but.*

*Harrison thought he and Dad would explore together, but on the second day **dad decides** to go fishing.*

The sentence is still wrong, even now. That *dad* should be *Dad.* That *decides* is wrong too. This story is being told in past tense, and *decides* is a present tense verb. It should be *decided.*

*"You can explore," he **tells** Harrison.*

Tells is wrong because it is a present tense verb. It should be *told.*

"I might get lost." **S***aid Harrison.*

The full stop should be a comma. *Said* should be *said.*

*"You can't get lost while you can see Captain Cash's Cove***", ***Dad* ***told****.*

Told is wrong. It has to have a word after it. That could be *him* or *Harrison*. If it was changed to *said* it would be okay.
The comma before *Dad* should come before the quote marks, not after them.

Harrison ***wondered around*** *the island. He got hungry.*

The second word is wrong. *Wondered* should be *wandered.*

There's something else wrong there too. Because this is an important part of the story, it needs to be made more interesting. What does Harrison see and do while he's wandering about? He's supposed to be exploring, so what does he stop to look at?

"I'll go back to ***dad,****" he thought.*

That *dad* should be *Dad.* Also, Harrison is thinking, not speaking, so there should not be quote marks.

"I just have to find Captain ***Cod's*** *Cove."*

There shouldn't be quote marks because Harrison is thinking. Also, there's an inconsistency. The name of the cove has changed from *Captain Cash's Cove* to *Captain Cod's Cove*.

Harrison looked up at the sun. He knew how to find east. Was the cove east or west?

This piece is all right as it is.

He tried to remember if Mr ***Pickering****, who* ***bought*** *them to the island, had said anything about that.*

Here is another consistency error. It was Mr *Pilgrim* who brought them to the island, not Mr *Pickering.*
The word *bought* should be *brought.*

"OK, I'll climb up a tree and see if ***I,"*** *he* ***yelled****.*

This sentence has words missing after *I.* Also, there's no reason for Harrison to yell these words.

He ***climbs*** *the tree and saw the camp.*

The tense is wrong. *Climbs* is present tense and *saw* is past tense.
Also, once again we have an important part of the story that hasn't enough detail and excitement.

"That was an adventure, ***dad,*** *he* ***complained*** *when he got back.*

This should be *Dad.* There's a quote mark missing before *he complained* and *complained* is the wrong word anyway. Also, again this is too sudden.

So, how did you go with the editing? Let's look at the story with those spelling and punctuation mistakes fixed.

"Mr Pilgrim will take us to the island on Friday and pick us up a week later," Dad said. "We'll have a whole seven days to explore all the bays."

"Sounds excellent!" Harrison said.

Harrison thought he and Dad would explore together, but on the second day Dad decided to go fishing. "You can explore," he told Harrison.

"I might get lost," said Harrison.

"You can't get lost while you can see Captain Cash's Cove," Dad told him.

**Harrison wandered around the island. He got hungry.*

I'll go back to Dad, he thought. I just have to find Captain Cash's Cove.

Harrison looked up at the sun. He knew how to find east. Was the cove east or west?

He tried to remember if Mr Pilgrim, who brought them to the island, had said anything about that.

OK, I'll climb up a tree and see if I can see any landmarks, he decided.

OR

"OK, I'll climb up a tree and see if I can see any landmarks," he said aloud.

**He climbed the tree and saw the camp.*

"That was an adventure, Dad," he said when he got back.

This editing has fixed the spelling and punctuation mistakes, but it still isn't an awesome story. The bits marked with an asterisk * need quite a bit more detail and some exciting action. After all, Harrison tells Dad it was an adventure and really, it wasn't.

How do you make it into an adventure? Remember the three questions Awesome Authors ask themselves?

Okay, what *would* really happen?

Most likely, Dad wouldn't let Harrison go off on his own. This is a deserted island, but most dads don't let their kids go off in a strange environment. There could be sharks, crocodiles, green ants, stonefish, rips, undertow, cliffs, stinging trees and goodness knows what else. Dad would probably tell Harrison they could go fishing and then explore.

That's what would probably happen, but it doesn't make much of a story, does it?

Dad and Harrison go on holiday to a deserted island. Dad won't let Harrison wander off so he watches Dad fishing.

Okay, if what would *really* happen is too ordinary to make a good story, what is the most interesting thing that could happen? What would your readers want to have happen?

Think about it and write down some ideas. Then write the best ones into the story.

Genres

Genres are kinds of stories. There are heaps of different genres. You can even have cross-genre stories (which use two genres at the same time) and sub-genre stories (which use a branch of a genre).

Here are some to pick from. You can probably think of others.

Adventure	Fantasy adventure	Problem stories
Animal stories	Quest fantasy	Realism
Cat stories	Fantasy realism	Romance
Dog stories	Urban fantasy	School stories
Pony stories	Fairy tales	Boarding school
Ballet stories	Farm stories	Theatre school
Career stories	Ghost stories	Science fiction
Circus stories	Graphic novel	Space stories
Comic book	Historical stories	Sports stories
Crime	Historical adventure	Cricket
Detective	Horror	Football
Diary stories	Humour	Swimming
Dragon stories	Letter stories	Steampunk
Drama	Mermaid stories	Superhero
Family stories	Monster stories	Theatre stories
Family adventure	Mystery	Time travel
Fantasy	Paranormal stories	Travel stories
Domestic fantasy	Picaresque stories	Verse stories

Ms Tiggy's Beginnings

1. The roses were velvety and thorny in equal parts.
2. "It's a castle!" said Beatrice in astonishment.
3. "Daisies? It eats *daisies?*" said Zac.
4. Ruby had been missing for two days now.
5. "Gotcha!" gloated Gareth.
6. The apple was covered in ants.
7. When Dad said we were going into space we all stared.
8. "You can have one, that's all," said Jack.
9. Skating was a lot more difficult than Josh expected.
10. Miss Perry's garden was overgrown with thistles.
11. The wasps poured from their nest.
12. The egg didn't look like the others.
13. Did we have to have jam sandwiches again?
14. Christie said the toy was a squid.
15. Ash and Mica said they would make the biscuits.
16. The green coat had woolly bobbles on the belt.
17. On the second day of our holiday it started to rain.
18. *Dear Clara, why did you steal my kayak?*
19. Stonemasons' sons did not go to school. Stephen knew that.
20. Robert lived in the attic of a tall grey house in London.
21. More than anything, Ellie wanted an earring with a skull on it.
22. "It's no good," said Lindsay, looking at the smashed boat.
23. "Go back!" yelled Ming, waving wildly.
24. Grapes were usually green, weren't they?

25. *Happy New Year*! screamed the banner, but it wasn't happy for Bella.
26. How many trees were in this forest anyway?
27. "Do you like caterpillars?" asked Davie.
28. The desert stretched on and on.
29. No one ever saw my friend Kit, but I knew he was there.
30. "For the last time, I did *not* kidnap you!"
31. Ponies are hard work.
32. I looked up at the dinosaur.
33. "He was here just a moment ago," said Imogen.
34. "Help! He's getting away!"
35. The clouds spread below our feet like ice cream hills.
36. It was so quiet I thought I heard the stars fizzing softly.
37. "Wait for me!" Jillie hopped along on one foot as she tried to get her shoe on.
38. Dragons don't live in suburban gardens.
39. "No more ghosts," said the mayor, thumping his fist on the desk.
40. If I could just kick that goal I might make the team.
41. These days, everyone lived in tree houses.
42. Elliot had taken a wrong turn at soft furnishings and now he was lost in the biggest shop he had ever seen.
43. The last car ever produced on Earth is now in a museum.
44. Is it possible to lose a teddy bear for three whole years?
45. The monster had feet shaped like shoeboxes.
46. I never expected to meet my great great great-grandad.
47. Flora set down the handcart and rubbed her blistered hands.
48. The streamers stretched and tore as the ship pulled away from the quay.
49. Mr Hanson plonked his fingers down on the keys and began to play.
50. *My uncle is a vampire*, wrote Tom in careful black letters.
51. "If you think I'm going into that cave, you're nuts," said Grace.
52. The new house looked worse than our old one.

Wow! That's enough for me to write a new story every week for a whole year!

Ms Tiggy's Characters

Here are 52 characters to use for your own stories.

1. A dragon named Bleep
2. A talking duck
3. A cross clown
4. Twin unicorns
5. A clumsy boy named Blake
6. A girl named Annie who hates dancing
7. A pirate's parrot
8. A clever cat
9. A boy who is much taller than his friends
10. A girl whose aunt is younger than she is
11. A giraffe with blue spots
12. A 19th Century servant boy
13. A convict girl named Lucy
14. A time-traveller from the future
15. An alien cat
16. An escaped slave
17. A girl whose brother is missing
18. A boy whose mother is a teacher
19. A girl who lives with her cousins
20. A magic doll
21. A boy who is bad at sport
22. A princess from the past
23. A child superhero
24. A boy lost in a computer game
25. A girl lost in the desert
26. A boy who wakes up and finds out he's a fish
27. A girl who has to do a project with her enemy
28. A schoolgirl who is really a fairy
29. An artist whose pictures come to life
30. A girl who grows giant pumpkins
31. A girl who hates shopping
32. A boy who wants a dog and gets a cat instead
33. A monster that lives under the bed
34. A ghost that lives in a football

35. A boy trapped in a sinking ship
36. A granny who flies a balloon
37. A merboy who wants to go to a normal school
38. The spider that lives behind a calendar
39. An orphan from the 1930s
40. A pony named King
41. A prince no one listens to
42. A lonely cow
43. A cave monster
44. A possum that lives in the barn
45. A city fairy
46. A boy whose best friend is a robot
47. The cabin boy of a spaceship
48. A girl whose mother won the lottery
49. An invisible boy
50. A girl whose twin is better at everything
51. A girl who doesn't like her babysitter
52. A boy who fights a fire

Mr Bock's Glossary

Action- things that happen visibly in a story

Adjective- ***ad**-jec-tiv*- word that describes a noun. Red, big, pretty, silky, and wet are adjectives

Adverb- word that describes a verb. Quickly, angrily, well, darkly are adverbs

Antagonist- *an-**tag**-on-ist*- the person whose aim is the opposite of the main character's

Author- ***or**-ther*- person who creates stories with words

Back-story- things that happened before the story begins

Blurb- a bit about the story so readers know if they want to read it

Character- ***carr**-ac-ter*- living person or creature in a story. Also personality

Character development- parts of a story that make a character change and grow

Conjunction- word such as and, but, because, or which that links two parts of a sentence

Description- words telling how things look, sound or appear

Dialogue- ***die**-a-log*- conversation in a story

Editing- working on a story to make it more awesome

Exposition- *ex-pos-**ish**-on.* Information to explain things to readers

Family Realism- a story based around families that *could* happen

Fantasy- a story in which things happen that couldn't happen in our reality

Genre- ***zhon**-ra*- a kind of story, such a sport story, romance, western or fantasy

Graphic novel- ***graff**-ic **nov**-ell* - story told in captions, pictures and speech balloons

Narrative- ***narr**-a-tiv*- the part of a story that tells us what is happening

Noun- a naming word such as cat, table, John, star, voice, wind

Pace- the speed at which important things happen in a story

Paragraph- ***parra**-graff* - piece of a story that deals with one idea

Picaresque- ***pick-a-esk***- a story without much plot where characters move around a lot

Plot- what happens to the characters in a story

Point of View- the way a story is told

Protagonist- *pro-**tag**-on-ist*- the main character in a story

Punctuation- *punct-you-**aish**-on*- marks such as commas and question marks that make stories easier to read

Research- searching for information to make stories more accurate or believable

Scene- part of a story that happens to the same people at the same place and time

Science Fiction- stories of things that can't happen yet with plots based on science

Sentence- a group of words containing a subject, an object and a verb. It begins with a capital letter and mostly ends with a full stop, a question mark or an exclamation mark

Setting- where a story takes place

Style- the way things are written, including the choice of words

Synopsis- *sin-**opp**-sis-* a short version of the story which includes the ending

Tense- the way a story is told, whether it is happening now or was in the past

Thesaurus- *th-ee-**saw**-us-* a book that explains synonyms and antonyms

Verb- an action word. Run, talk, swim, go, live are verbs

Vocabulary- *vo-**cab**-you-larry* - the range of words an awesome author knows

Voice- whether a story is told *by* a character or *about* a character

Go and be Awesome, Author!

Remember-

Start with ideas, like Arthur.

Add some imagination, like Matilda.

Ask the right questions, like Caspar.

Organise things properly, like Sakura.

Invent memorable characters… like Hieronymous Beetle

Use the best words to write about them, like Mr Bock.

Come up with handy lists, like Ms Tiggy

And take a lot of interest in life, like Jackbeard.

And in the end you'll be an utterly awesome author…

…and now you know

www.ingramcontent.com/pod-product-compliance
Ingram Content Group UK Ltd.
Pitfield, Milton Keynes, MK11 3LW, UK
UKHW050614260726
13967UKWH00008B/2865

9 781304 955807